M000310668

Transformational Grace

*A language of the transforming power
of God's grace through poetry*

SANDRA HADLAND

Trilogy Christian Publishers A Wholly Owned Subsidiary of Trinity Broadcasting Network 2442 Michelle Drive Tustin, CA 92780

Copyright © 2018 by Sandra Hadland

All Scripture quotations, unless otherwise noted, taken from THE HOLY BIBLE, NEW INTERNATIONAL VERSION®, NIV® Copyright © 1973, 1978, 1984, 2011 by Biblica, Inc.® Used by permission. All rights reserved worldwide.

All rights reserved, including the right to reproduce this book or portions thereof in any form whatsoever. For information, address Trilogy Christian Publishing Rights Department, 2442 Michelle Drive, Tustin, Ca 92780.

First Trilogy Christian Publishing hardcover edition May 2018 Trilogy Christian Publishing/ TBN and colophon are trademarks of Trinity Broadcasting Network.

For information about special discounts for bulk purchases, please contact Trilogy Christian Publishing.

Manufactured in the United States of America

10 9 8 7 6 5 4 3 2 1

Library of Congress Cataloging-in-Publication Data is available.

ISBN 978-1-64088-089-4 (Paperback)
SBN 978-1-64088-090-0 (ebook)

Foreword

How many times in life have we lived through an experience, and once the experience is over, we realized that we could summarize the experience as an experience *"where you could not see the forest for the trees"*? On the other hand, when was the last time you experienced something, and when the experience was over you realized in hindsight you had twenty-twenty vision? Drawing from the real life experiences that are contained in the *Book of Psalms*, and using her own life experiences and insights as a committed and dedicated Christian, Sandra Hadland has magically used her poetic abilities to help her audience see the forest through the trees, and use spiritual insight to develop spiritual foresight.

Transformational Grace is a book that is destined to become a "must have" for anyone who is serious about Christian discipleship and who is concerned about developing a deep and meaningful personal relationship with the Lord. Sandra's determination to know the Lord on a personal basis, and to see how the Holy Spirit uses the Holy Scriptures to provide spiritual illumination to the lives of the believer, has resulted in a unique and rich presentation of poetry that will enrich and transform the lives of people for years to come.

Dr. William B. Sutton, III, Pastor
First Baptist Church of Stratford
Stratford, Connecticut

Preface

"Transformational Grace" is about an awakening realization of one's journey through life to purpose. It identifies with our inmost times of hurt, of pain and of frustration, while offering incites of hope to work through a process that will ultimately guide us into purpose. Through the desire and willingness to submit and accept God's grace, we learn to identify with His will. As a result, a transforming relationship and trust is born while embracing the One who has our best interest at heart while, offering only the best.

"Transformational Grace" lays bare the very soul, it challenges and defies the carnal nature of one's being. It questions circumstances and conditions of people of all walks of life, be they people who gravitate to negativism, and resolve to accept paralyzation and defeat, or persons who believe they have it made, yet feel a void they cannot fill. It awakens the subconscious to the truth that, on the road to purpose, trials and tribulations are necessary implementations for the refinement of character.

Although at times, one's present condition can be brought about by oneself and not necessarily by others, the result thereof is nevertheless determined by one's attitude and reaction to their present condition. Will they come to terms with the reality of their present condition, and moreover, what will they do about it? The answer to this question is an act of our choice. *Transformational* Grace was written from the depths of the soul in order to identify, inspire, incite hope and ultimately provoke a lasting, authentic change that can only be produced through the Transforming Grace of Christ.

It is my hope and prayer that everyone who takes the time to digest the words written on these pages will come to a newness of heart and mind in their journey of life. There are so many who desire the prize without wanting to go through the process. The real prize, however, is only achieved when we run our race. I truly believe God uniquely designs us with a purpose that is distinct to each individual and no one else. Our lives can line up with our purpose in and through His "Transformational Grace," after all; it is a matter of our choice!

Sandra Hadland

Moments to reflect, meditate, and respond
Suggestions from the author

After each poem, take a moment to reflect, meditate and respond to the poem and scripture. You may use the reflection sheet found after each poem to make your entries.

*Finally, having completed your moments of reflection, meditation and response to each poem and corresponding scripture, I invite you to pay close attention in order to discern footprints of the Holy Spirit, be intentional to His guidance in your life. You may use the summary sheets found at the end of the poem collection to make a **summary of your collective findings**.*

Sandra Hadland.

Look To The Source

When your heart is breaking, look to the source

When you don't understand, look to the source

When you can't find a way out, look to the source

When life throws you a curveball, look to the source

When you've done all you can do, look to the source

When you feel you can't go any further, look to the source

When everything is at a stand-still, look to the source

When the bottom falls out, still look to the source

When it all makes no sense, surrender totally
and allow the source to work for you.

"I lift up my eyes to the hills – Where does my help come from?
My help comes from the Lord, the maker of heaven and
earth." Psalm 121:1-2

POEM REFLECTION
Look To The Source

How did this poem and scripture speak to me?

PRAYER: Holy Spirit, make me aware of the changes needed in my life, then give me the mind and strength to follow through. Thank you, Holy Spirit, for your footprints.

LIST CHANGES TO BE MADE
**Revealed areas of my life by the
Holy Spirit to make changes**

A Letter To God

Dear God, I don't quite know what to say

I've tried everything else and I don't know what to do

They say if I talk to you, you will hear me

I'm no holy person and I have nothing to give to you

But I figure, I have nothing to lose and
it might be worth a chance

I hurt so much, I can't even cry

If you're really there God, make me feel
something other than pain

Let me know what it is to be loved, to be
wanted, to be saved, even from myself

Sometimes I close my eyes and wish it were only a
dream, but when I open my eyes the reality is the same

Is there some sense to life after all? Is
there a way of finding out?

Please God, lift me from the chains of despair,
give me hope to hold on till my change comes

Open my eyes that I might see clearly, my ears that I might hear you, and my heart to receive my change.

Until then God, please keep me for
I fear I cannot keep myself

Thank you God for listening and I
hope to hear from you soon.

Forever Grateful,
Me

"Call to me and I will answer you and tell you great and unsearchable things you do not know." Jeremiah 33:3

POEM REFLECTION
A Letter To God

How did this poem and scripture speak to me?

PRAYER: Holy Spirit, make me aware of the changes needed in my life, then give me the mind and strength to follow through. Thank you, Holy Spirit, for your footprints.

LIST CHANGES TO BE MADE **Revealed areas of my life by the** **Holy Spirit to make changes**

A Cry For Help

In deep dark silence there is a cry

A cry for help but who can truly know- the
pain and anguish from deep within

From the depths of my soul, a language is
spoken, but only those who experience my pain
can truly understand and identify with me

I've tried all that I know to do, but nothing works

Pain and anguish melts into frustration

If only someone can truly see, but no one does

I put on the best possible front to cover my pain;
day after day I hope for my season of change

Instead, helplessness and despair appear to be my only gain

I'm at a place where I'm not in control, I
ponder in my mind if it's worth going on

I recall shattered and unmet dreams,
thwarted efforts and crushed hopes

With a broken spirit I muster from my
soul, one final cry for help

Just then… out of nowhere appeared a ray
of hope, my innermost being struggled and
strained but I grabbed on for dear life

Closing my eyes and giving it my all, I
shouted; Yes! I'm willing to go on. At that very
moment I knew, my change had come.

"Hear my prayer, O Lord; let my cry for help come to you. Do
not hide your face from me when I am in distress. Turn your
ear to me; when I call, answer me quickly." Psalm 102:1-2

POEM REFLECTION
A Cry For Help

How did this poem and scripture speak to me?

_____
_____
_____
_____
_____
_____
_____
_____
_____
_____

PRAYER: Holy Spirit, make me aware of the changes needed in my life, then give me the mind and strength to follow through. Thank you, Holy Spirit, for your footprints.

LIST CHANGES TO BE MADE
**Revealed areas of my life by the
Holy Spirit to make changes**

_____
_____
_____
_____
_____
_____
_____
_____
_____

The Beauty Of The Rose

I stare in awe as I contemplate the rose

Its beauty, sweet fragrance, and proud pronounced petals

How awesome, powerful, and breathtaking
is this flower when we stop to consider its
journey, in order to become a rose,

Its beginning is meshed with the soil of the ground
where given adequate positioning, nourishment,
and atmospheric conditions, it flourishes

Day after day the Gardener tends with love to
his garden and waits patiently for his prize
As the rose begins its journey through time
meeting obstacles at many turns in the process

Each thorn represents a trial, tribulation or obstacle
it must overcome, yet to become all it is meant to
be, with the help of the Gardener, it perseveres

Over time, with roots firmly rooted in place, it stands as a
grand bush secured in the knowledge that it will overcome

Soon it begins its metamorphosis; all that was
in the beginning of the rose, hidden from
the naked eye suddenly becomes a bud

The bud grows larger and larger until finally
it is ready to be revealed, a beautiful rose

Withstanding every hardship, from within the
journey of thorns, the elements stood through
the protected stems and branches

To the naked eye the thorns seem insurmountable,
challenging and impossible to overcome

Yet the inner structure, potential, and goal of the
end result is already purposed from within

Now we gaze upon the end result, a beauty of grace to
behold, whose petals stand firm and strong, a testimony
to the care, love and affection of the Gardener, and the
patient trust and perseverance of the metamorphosis.

Finally it serves its purpose bringing beauty,
joy, and love while giving a sweet aroma to the
nostrils of all; "The beauty of the rose."

"No, in all these things we are more than conquerors through
him who loved us. For I am convinced that neither death
nor life, neither angels nor demons, neither the present nor
the future, nor any powers, neither height nor depth, nor
anything else in all creation, will be able to separate us from
the love of God that is in Christ Jesus our Lord." Romans
8:37-39

POEM REFLECTION
The Beauty Of The Rose

How did this poem and scripture speak to me?

PRAYER: Holy Spirit, make me aware of the changes needed in my life, then give me the mind and strength to follow through. Thank you, Holy Spirit, for your footprints.

LIST CHANGES TO BE MADE
**Revealed areas of my life by the
Holy Spirit to make changes**

Life Is A Journey

Life is a journey we all must take

Though, on occasions, we don't know which way to go

We chart our course, follow our dreams,
and at times ride the winds of success

Touching lives as we travel one step at a time

Within each step numerous challenges arise

The question is: should I focus on the
challenge, or my response to the quest?

Though circumstances, situations, conditions,
and people, individually or collectively,
make my response an awesome task

I must rise above every noise in the marketplace,
every challenge not favoring my good

I must press to reach beyond my own limitations
and cling to unlimited resources

I must look as I have never looked before and seek
to claim my place for which I am purposed

Like a sweet smelling rose who has overcome
every difficulty and achieved its purpose

I must overcome the discouragement of each
thorn of every branch and instead
continue to be nourished, grow and bloom

I must overcome every obstacle including myself and
finally, send forth a sweet smelling aroma to my maker

"Brothers, I do not consider myself yet to have taken hold of it. But one thing I do: Forgetting what is behind and straining to what is ahead, I press on toward the goal to win the prize for which God has called me heavenward in Christ Jesus." Philippians 3:13-14

POEM REFLECTION
Life Is A Journey

How did this poem and scripture speak to me?

PRAYER: Holy Spirit, make me aware of the changes needed in my life, then give me the mind and strength to follow through. Thank you, Holy Spirit, for your footprints.

LIST CHANGES TO BE MADE
**Revealed areas of my life by the
Holy Spirit to make changes**

The Naked Truth

In our world today as in time past, there is
much controversy about the word "truth"

Some people make this claim in connection with untold
situations pertaining to their own interest; whatever
gives credence or leverage to what they imply

Truth, however, does not change, will not compromise,
stands the test of time, and eventually will eat up the lie

Does this mean that we must be afraid of truth? No, but
it means that truth should be respected and adhered to

Truth however always carries with it a price
but in the end emancipation is gained

We can live our lives always being trapped in a box by
lies, or emancipated by truth, and soar as the eagle

It is first a realization to take hold of, and then a
matter of choice, which will it be for you? In the
final analysis, the naked truth will always survive.

"…Jesus said, 'If you hold to my teaching, you are really my
disciples. Then you will know the truth, and the truth will set
you free.'" John 8:31-32

POEM REFLECTION
The Naked Truth

How did this poem and scripture speak to me?

_____

_____

_____

_____

_____

_____

_____

_____

_____

PRAYER: Holy Spirit, make me aware of the changes needed in my life, then give me the mind and strength to follow through. Thank you, Holy Spirit, for your footprints.

LIST CHANGES TO BE MADE
**Revealed areas of my life by the
Holy Spirit to make changes**

_____

_____

_____

_____

_____

_____

_____

_____

_____

The Journey

Life is a journey we all must tread

Though sometimes the road seem dim

It is then we look within our hearts to
the still small voice from within

To press through the tears until they subside

To ask for strength to carry us through

We press on through the weights, defying the
odds, believing each step of the way

That there is one who is on our side, in whom we can abide

He will dry our tears and order our steps

Till we, on our journey, overcome the odds

Then in retrospect examine ourselves
realizing an amazing growth

It is then we see the flower and smell the sweet aroma

An aroma produced only by overcoming the journey

Till then, we press on, knowing there is a prize

We won't give up, no matter the cost

We will press on to the very end until victory is won.

"…we also rejoice in our sufferings, because we know that suffering produces perseverance; perseverance character; and character, hope." Romans 5:3-4

POEM REFLECTION
The Journey

How did this poem and scripture speak to me?

PRAYER: Holy Spirit, make me aware of the changes needed in my life, then give me the mind and strength to follow through. Thank you, Holy Spirit, for your footprints.

LIST CHANGES TO BE MADE
Revealed areas of my life by the
Holy Spirit to make changes

Hope

Oh that I can find myself within a world so cruel

A world that has damaged my hopes,
my dreams and my very soul

When will the time come to heal? To
move beyond the pangs of pain

Pain so deep I am weighed down and have become thin

Thin in my hopes, my dreams, my outlook,
surroundings, and faith in humankind

Where is the help to bring me through?
Help that I might live again

I look around and darkness is all I see

Oh for a caring hand to reach out to me

My wounds so deep, they crippled my soul;
there must be a way to gain control

Will someone please hear my cry, lest in
this dungeon I shall truly die?

My arms are outstretched; my eyes grow dim,
they try to cry but tears cease to come

Though swollen eyelids, they squint to see any chance
of hope, a change that certainly must be for me

My body grows weary, my heart beats faint - suddenly,
with a glimmer of hope, a voice whispers, you shall see!!

"Why are you downcast, O my soul? Why so disturbed within me? Put your hope in God, for I will yet praise him, my savior and my God." Psalm 42:11

POEM REFLECTION
Hope

How did this poem and scripture speak to me?

_____

_____

_____

_____

_____

_____

_____

_____

_____

PRAYER: Holy Spirit, make me aware of the changes needed in my life, then give me the mind and strength to follow through. Thank you, Holy Spirit, for your footprints.

LIST CHANGES TO BE MADE
**Revealed areas of my life by the
Holy Spirit to make changes**

_____

_____

_____

_____

_____

_____

_____

_____

_____

_____

My Guide

Out of the miry pit I rise to tell my story of my guide
Although at times, I could not see
My guide was always by my side and would not let me be
Through trials thick and thin he charted my
course, always faithful and forgiving
Always willing to bring me back on course
With patience and longsuffering His grace endures
His love so perfect you could depend on and be secure

I grew to trust Him taking baby steps in stride,
until I was secured with Him by my side
I rise to tell you there is a plan, a plan
for your life, divinely inspired
Oh that you would let go and let God
That the Potter might fashion and
form you into his desired plan
I know it's frightening, not to be in charge
But what good is a leader who is
inadequate to accomplish the task

I know a guide who makes no mistakes, have charted
your course and determined it by His grace

A guide who loves you unconditionally,
one who has paid the ultimate price
To bring you in the way of knowledge and
truth, and to give you everlasting life
His name is Jesus, The Lord, King of
Kings, and Lord of Lords
Master, Teacher, Friend, and even
The Beginning and the End
How can you lose with such a guide?
I dare you to try and walk with Him by your side.

"But the pot he was shaping from the clay was marred in his hands; so the potter formed it into another pot, shaping it as seemed best to him." Jeremiah 18:4

POEM REFLECTION
My Guide

How did this poem and scripture speak to me?

PRAYER: Holy Spirit, make me aware of the changes needed in my life, then give me the mind and strength to follow through. Thank you, Holy Spirit, for your footprints.

LIST CHANGES TO BE MADE
**Revealed areas of my life by the
Holy Spirit to make changes**

A Valley Of Indecision

Lord, I'm tired of being in this place; I
ask myself, what is going on?
I feel my heart pound, I break out in
a cold sweat, I pray and I cry
What is the problem? I ask, what am I
doing wrong, or not doing at all?
Your Word, I believe, is firmly hid in my heart, but yet
I'm in the valley of indecision
Something is wrong what could it be?
I must dig until I finally see

Enlighten me that I might see - surely in
your plan for me this must be
Help me to stand firm, and waver not
To move in your will, and receive my fair lot
Forsaking myself and clinging only to
you, help me, and this I shall do
Abundant life is your will for me –
Open my eyes that I will see

Now my eyes are opened – and new things I see
– I was not aware fear had its grips in me
Grips in my mind with shadows of doubt, so
subtle - there seemed to be no way out
Intruding my mind – this enemy came as a thief
- to steal my peace, and take away my shout
Moved with intention with you by my side
I stood my guard and with the word fought the lie

With lashes intense, precise and secure, fear
lost the battle and was there no more
Crippled no more by fear in my mind –
I move forward claiming all things that are mine
I don't have all the answers but I know One who does
For me now - The valley of indecision is a faint memory!

"… God did not give us a spirit of timidity, but a spirit of power, of love and of self discipline." 2 Timothy 1:7

POEM REFLECTION
A Valley Of Indecision

How did this poem and scripture speak to me?

PRAYER: Holy Spirit, make me aware of the changes needed in my life, then give me the mind and strength to follow through. Thank you, Holy Spirit, for your footprints.

LIST CHANGES TO BE MADE
**Revealed areas of my life by the
Holy Spirit to make changes**

Miracle Of The Dock

The dock whose steel and concrete pillars are
fastened into the depths of the ocean
Withstands the raging storms and
billows of tumultuous waves
Though angry winds twirl and howl and
violent seas rise high and beat against it
Its stability will break and calm the billows of every
swelling wave, while tumultuous currents from
beneath dislodge harmful debris from its depths

After the storm has subsided and
passed, the dock remains intact
Although its pronounced stance may show signs of warfare
Nevertheless, its firm demeanor prevails and brings change
There on the horizon, as far as the eyes could see
Unseemly debris is a visibility
No longer unseen, but seen to the naked eye, those
things which were hidden beneath the surface

Suddenly our physical eyes are replaced with spiritual eyes
Our understanding is enlightened and we can see
Like this unwavering dock, our stand on the
word of God will undoubtedly try us
It will stir up and shake within us
everything that is not of Him
In every step of the way, He is our
strength when we are weak
He is our eyes when we cannot see, our
hope when all hope is gone

Our "ALL IN ALL" - THE GREAT "I AM."
Standing firmly in place, and anchored in the Word,
the storms pass over, and we emerge victorious
Harmful debris from within us surface
And God's barge, by removing debris, brings deliverance
I am being transformed by His Grace day after day!!

"...My son, do not make light of the Lord's discipline, and do not lose heart when he rebukes you, because the Lord disciplines those he loves..." Hebrews 12:5-6

POEM REFLECTION
Miracle Of The Dock

How did this poem and scripture speak to me?

PRAYER: Holy Spirit, make me aware of the changes needed in my life, then give me the mind and strength to follow through. Thank you, Holy Spirit, for your footprints.

LIST CHANGES TO BE MADE
**Revealed areas of my life by the
Holy Spirit to make changes**

Realization

Reality, fantasy or denial!

Now my eyes have been opened, I have a
new perspective, a new realization

I understand I must be tried on what I profess

I now recognize the word of God to be TRUTH

The difference is, it must become truth in me

No longer is it intellectualism but it must germinate
within my mind and move into my heart

Then and only then will it be moved into action by me

No longer is it a dream or fantasy, nor
am I in a place of denial,
I must be able to determine the difference

Sorting through the many voices in my mind to
determine reality is to come to a realization of truth

Realization brings with it a consciousness, separating
its stance from illusion or contradiction to truth

This state of awareness dictates corresponding action

To deny the perspective of realization
brings a position of inactiveness

A place of danger, a targeted place for the enemy to attack

Although facing my reality from the
natural eye can be frightening

There is a place when rising above my five
senses brings me into another perspective,
a perspective where I can move by faith and not by sight

In this place, I have growth, there I am maturing
into the individual I am meant to be
Into the realization of, and acting upon, my purpose.

"Now faith is being sure of what we hope for and certain of
what we do not see." Hebrews 11:1

POEM REFLECTION
Realization

How did this poem and scripture speak to me?

_____
_____
_____
_____
_____
_____
_____
_____
_____
_____

PRAYER: Holy Spirit, make me aware of the changes needed in my life, then give me the mind and strength to follow through. Thank you, Holy Spirit, for your footprints.

LIST CHANGES TO BE MADE
**Revealed areas of my life by the
Holy Spirit to make changes**

_____
_____
_____
_____
_____
_____
_____
_____
_____
_____

Who Am I?

To live my life by my own understanding is
to conclude that I know what is best for me
at all times; arrogant and self-centered.
This places me in a very vulnerable and toxic
position whether I am aware of it or not
Did I just evolve? If so, from what and for what or, is there
a divine plan for my life, with a specific reason and purpose?
Not finding out from the Word of God who I am
is to spend my entire lifetime as an imposter

Made in the image and likeness of God translates that I am
made expressly to reflect the nature of God to the extent
of the capacity given me in thought, speech, and action.
To the contrary, life puts all kinds of claims on who I am
I am a person, an individual, a human being who
identifies with family, friends and society at large
Within this framework, everyone plays a different
beat and expects a certain march from me
Inside my soul, how awful is the conflict within me
when I try to march to everyone's beat but my own
Senseless efforts with no real meaning and no
real values are to be had; they go against the very
grain of who I really am as a spiritual being

I must rise to the occasion no matter
what, not for fame, nor for fortune
Not for popularity, or for the safeness of this world
I must look carefully into the Word of God and allow my
actions to reflect Him by modeling the life of Christ

God said I am made to reflect his thought pattern, reflect
the kind of words he speak, and reflect his actions
I must be still while the potter forms and shapes me,
even shaping me again as seems good to the potter
When I am released by the potter, I shall be a
jewel to behold, ready to walk in my purpose.
I must surrender my carnal nature and be willing to put
the imposter to death so that God might rebuild and refine
me, then and only then will I truly know "Who AM I"

"Then God said, Let us make man [humankind] in our
image, in our likeness…" Genesis 1:26

POEM REFLECTION
Who Am I?

How did this poem and scripture speak to me?

PRAYER: Holy Spirit, make me aware of the changes needed in my life, then give me the mind and strength to follow through. Thank you, Holy Spirit, for your footprints.

LIST CHANGES TO BE MADE
**Revealed areas of my life by the
Holy Spirit to make changes**

A Blessed Promise

Sing praises to our God
For He has given us a promise
A promise that we belong to Him
Though we have strayed and forsaken Him
Yet will His providence remain upon us
For He is faithful and true and cannot lie
He who has promised is able to fulfill every vow

Rejoice, O soul, and again, rejoice
The days of mourning shall surely come to an end
For the Lord, our God shall bring His promises to pass

Through deep pangs of intercession,
we will sing praises to our God
For yet will our God restore us
Though we went a far distance and left Him
Yet He will remain faithful to us

Oh sing praises all who mourn in the dust
Lift up your eyes and see
For that which was promised shall surely come to pass
For the mouth of the Lord has spoken it

Rejoice, Rejoice, and again I say, Rejoice!

"Let us hold unswervingly to the hope we profess, for he who
promised is faithful." Hebrews 10:23

POEM REFLECTION
A Blessed Promise

How did this poem and scripture speak to me?

| |
| |
| |
| |
| |
| |
| |
| |
| |
| |

PRAYER: Holy Spirit, make me aware of the changes needed in my life, then give me the mind and strength to follow through. Thank you, Holy Spirit, for your footprints.

LIST CHANGES TO BE MADE
**Revealed areas of my life by the
Holy Spirit to make changes**

| |
| |
| |
| |
| |
| |
| |
| |
| |

The Miracle Of A Seed

A seed contains the fulfillment of all it's purposed to be

But on its own or by itself, it's nothing more than just a seed

To gaze upon it in its infant stage is to see
nothing more than what is natural, a seed

Then comes along a helper, one of faith,
vision, purpose, patience, and care

One who realizes the potential of a seed when
given the right circumstances and conditions
to succeed, and offers a helping hand

In the right season, he plants the seed in climate and
conditions suitable for its sustenance, care and growth

Over time, with constant care, the seed
begins to germinate where it is planted

Behind the scene, and at work, a
metamorphosis is taking place

The seed becomes a small plant; the helper being filled
with love and excitement guards and protects the plant
from agents of abuse that threatens its survival

While nurturing the plant in its tender stage, the
helper continues to wait with love, patience and care

Soon, the plant becomes a strong tree whose branches
produces much blossoms and eventually bring forth an
abundance of fruit giving many, many more seeds

Seeds of which to the naked eye are just seeds, but
to those of vision, seeds filled with potential

Are you a helper who recognizes the potential
of a seed? Can you see its worth?
Or do you only see a seed?

The Miracle of a Seed!

"As the rain and the snow come down from heaven, and do
not return to it without watering the earth and making it bud
and flourish, so that it yields seed for the sower and bread for
the eater. So is my word that goes out from my mouth: It will
not return to me empty, but will accomplish what I desire
and achieve the purpose for which I sent it." Isaiah 55:10-11

POEM REFLECTION
The Miracle Of A Seed

How did this poem and scripture speak to me?

PRAYER: Holy Spirit, make me aware of the changes needed in my life, then give me the mind and strength to follow through. Thank you, Holy Spirit, for your footprints.

LIST CHANGES TO BE MADE
**Revealed areas of my life by the
Holy Spirit to make changes**

Come Into The Deep

Don't toddle in the shallow waters, come into the deep

Give me your hand and I will guide you

Keep your eyes on me and do not stray

It is I who have called you – with a plan already in place

No one can take away the blessings I have ordained for you

But, not being in position to claim them
makes it possible to forfeit them

I know your struggles, I know your pain

I know your ups and I know your downs

Clothe your spirit with my promises every morning

Conceive them in your mind, believe them in
your heart, and act them out in your daily life

Your blessings from the supernatural into the natural are like
making deposits into a bank and later making withdrawals

Know that this truth comes from the One who cannot lie

Now come out into the deep with your face as
a flint, don't turn to the left or to the right

Dare to trust me and see if I won't turn
your circumstances around.
I - Love -You!

"Do not merely listen to the word, and so deceive yourselves.
Do what it says." James 1:22

POEM REFLECTION
Come Into The Deep

How did this poem and scripture speak to me?

PRAYER: Holy Spirit, make me aware of the changes needed in my life, then give me the mind and strength to follow through. Thank you, Holy Spirit, for your footprints.

LIST CHANGES TO BE MADE
Revealed areas of my life by the
Holy Spirit to make changes

Stand Firm In The Storm

No matter what the enemy throws your way, stand firm

God has already given you the victory to
every storm you may encounter

Although your emotions, your mind, and your physical
body cannot fathom the extent of the battle,

You are tired and cannot go any further, there are more
fighting for you than who are fighting against you

Hold on, walk in obedience, when you
have done all you can do, Stand!

Release the entire situations and those involved to God

He will fight the battle for you. Remember, He has not
brought you to the point of birth and will not deliver

He is counting on you to Stand

The intensity of the moment is just for a little while

The birth pains will soon be over, and that which
is brought forth will be glorious in His sight

When it is all said and done, people will
be edified and God Glorified

Now stand firm and see that which has been purposed
even before you were in your mother's womb

Stand firm, you can count on Him, He never
fails, and cannot lie – He will deliver!

"Do I bring to the moment of birth and not give delivery?"…
"Do I close up the womb when I bring to delivery? says your
God." Isaiah 66:9

POEM REFLECTION
Stand Firm In The Storm

How did this poem and scripture speak to me?

PRAYER: Holy Spirit, make me aware of the changes needed in my life, then give me the mind and strength to follow through. Thank you, Holy Spirit, for your footprints.

LIST CHANGES TO BE MADE
**Revealed areas of my life by the
Holy Spirit to make changes**

Make A Choice

Today, I make a choice and a conscious decision to release
every weight that presses me down, and every stronghold
that keeps me bound to the only one who can free me

Dear Lord, in your Grace, Mercy and Love, save me

Fight for me oh Lord, send the armies of
heaven to protect me, I belong to you

In the spiritual realm, I sense them gathering
together, they try their best to keep me
subdued, to tie my hands and my feet

They spew out untrue statements, and ban
together as one to imprison me

But you oh Lord have emancipated me, you have set me free

Let my feet be lifted up, and my wings spread wide,
my face is set as a flint looking only toward you

My mouth sings praises unto you, for you oh
God have ordained me to soar as an eagle

In the spiritual realm, you have snatched me
out of the traps that were set to destroy me

You have crowned me with your loving
kindness and granted me your favor

Only you oh God deserves all the praise,
all the glory and all the honor

Now my enemies will be made my footstool

In your Grace I ask, have mercy on them oh
my Lord as you have had mercy on me

"Finally, be strong in the Lord and in his mighty power...
For our struggle is not against flesh and blood, but against
the rulers, against the authorities, against the powers of this
dark world and against the spiritual forces of evil in the
heavenly realm. Therefore put on the full armor of God, so
that when the day of evil comes, you may be able to stand
your ground, and after you have done everything, to stand."
Ephesians 6:10-13

POEM REFLECTION
Make A Choice

How did this poem and scripture speak to me?

PRAYER: Holy Spirit, make me aware of the changes needed in my life, then give me the mind and strength to follow through. Thank you, Holy Spirit, for your footprints.

LIST CHANGES TO BE MADE
Revealed areas of my life by the
Holy Spirit to make changes

Destined To Soar As An Eagle

I was meant to identify with the eagle,
to soar in heights above
To see distances not designed for those
who cannot or will not soar
The eagle is aware of what is going on beneath
him but knows, it is not his place of residence
My wings are flapping to mount, my body
fixed to soar, there's no stopping me now
The chains that had me bound have all been released
I stare upward, my face as a flint; I soar
into the great wonder of the sky
A feeling of excitement, freedom, and
a new found courage beset me
There is no stopping me now
The taste of freedom is so natural, it's intoxicating
I see things I've never seen before and
didn't even know existed
I experience things I've never experienced before
Until now, I existed in a mistaken identity,
believing I could fly but trapped by situations,
conditions, people, and yes, even myself

In my new found freedom
I rise to take hold of that which is mine;
prepared for me from the beginning
To soar to heights, at first, not seen to the natural eye, that
place destined for me to fulfill the purpose set before me!

"...No eye has seen, no ear has heard, no mind has conceived what God has prepared for those who love him."
1 Corinthians 2:9

POEM REFLECTION
Destined To Soar As An Eagle

How did this poem and scripture speak to me?

PRAYER: Holy Spirit, make me aware of the changes needed in my life, then give me the mind and strength to follow through. Thank you, Holy Spirit, for your footprints.

LIST CHANGES TO BE MADE
**Revealed areas of my life by the
Holy Spirit to make changes**

Perception Of The Bitter Pill

Only an enlightening from above could
give me a new perspective on
the perception of the bitter pill
A perspective made so clear, it leaves
no possibility for coincidence
Now I reflect on the many trials over the course of life
and have come to the realization it was all in the plan
You put me in a choke, according to your own words
I did not understand, this choke was to make me free
A choke that placed me in a confined
place, a fiery furnace to be refined

You did it so I could be profitable for the
purpose for which I am made
The fire was so severe, it melted me down
It searched the innermost layers of my soul
Burning out the dross to make me whole
You stretched me, hammered me, and trained me
So as to be an ambassador of gold, of salt
for the earth, fit for the King

You placed from yourself, an anointing by the Holy Spirit
To accomplish your goal
You equipped and furnished me with what
is necessary to be radical for you
A stand to take that would not be colored by emotion
Or prejudiced by influence

To be strong and resistant to the pressures of the world
Firm and unyielding in truth
Vigorous, robust in character, strong in
faith, and to take a firm stand

Now I thank you for the perception of the bitter pill!

"...but we also rejoice in our sufferings, because we know that suffering produces perseverance; perseverance, character; and character, hope." Romans 5:3-4

POEM REFLECTION
Perception Of The Bitter Pill

How did this poem and scripture speak to me?

PRAYER: Holy Spirit, make me aware of the changes needed in my life, then give me the mind and strength to follow through. Thank you, Holy Spirit, for your footprints.

LIST CHANGES TO BE MADE
**Revealed areas of my life by the
Holy Spirit to make changes**

Grateful

Grateful is an understatement of how I truly feel
Words cannot adequately explain my joy
To place it mildly, miraculous is what comes to mind
No one but you Lord could do such awesome things for me
Miracle upon miracle, and yet some
Things too great for me to explain
How awesome you are in all your ways
My mouth shall proclaim it and my life live it

When the world tried to limit me with manmade rules
You said to be still until it is my time
You will take the lowly and produce
things too wonderful to know
In the final analysis it will be your show
Yes, they boast in their glory and manmade rules
But will not bow the knee to fulfill your core desire
They give a form of ambassadorship
But lack the true representation therein

Be still my child and let me work
I am building you brick by brick
With my own hands I determine your course
Oh how awesome is my God to me!

"Taste and see that the Lord is good; blessed is the [person]
who takes refuge in him." Psalm 34:8

POEM REFLECTION
Grateful

How did this poem and scripture speak to me?

| |
| |
| |
| |
| |
| |
| |
| |
| |
| |

PRAYER: Holy Spirit, make me aware of the changes needed in my life, then give me the mind and strength to follow through. Thank you, Holy Spirit, for your footprints.

LIST CHANGES TO BE MADE
**Revealed areas of my life by the
Holy Spirit to make changes**

| |
| |
| |
| |
| |
| |
| |
| |
| |

Favor Of The Divine

Be still my soul and rest, you have the favor of the Divine
Yes, your battle has already been won,
stand still, you will receive the prize
They present facts according to their agenda
But there is a place where I reside
That encourages me to trust in God and not man,
To trust in the One that has all power in His hands
Where, when human facts does not
make room for God's agenda
Human facts must bow to THE higher power
Be still, I say, you have the favor of the Divine
His favor has been poured out on me
His love ever so secure
Within this arena I've been purposed to dwell
Until it is my appointed time
I know, that time is here, my time to soar
The birthing process is at hand
Be still my soul and rest
You have the favor of the Divine!

"And we know that in all things God works for the good of those who love him, who have been called according to his purpose." Romans 8:28

POEM REFLECTION
Favor Of The Divine

How did this poem and scripture speak to me?

PRAYER: Holy Spirit, make me aware of the changes needed in my life, then give me the mind and strength to follow through. Thank you, Holy Spirit, for your footprints.

LIST CHANGES TO BE MADE
Revealed areas of my life by the
Holy Spirit to make changes

Torrents Of A Soaring River

My soul is bursting with joy
It overflows like a soaring river with a
force that no one can subside
All who come near will be drenched and saturated
Come; bathe in the exuberance of the overflow of the Lord
Make His name Glorious in all the earth
For He has saved me from all those who sought my harm
I sing praises; I bow down and worship
Him whose name is above all names
Joy besets me; Praise is like a torrent within me
I can't be still for my bones make music
My heart is like a drum, and my spirit
soars with sounds unimaginable
My feet move to the beat of my heart
And my hands dance in melodious sways
How can I tell you of such a joy? I can't really explain -
My body follows as my spirit leads
You fought the battle for me and gave me the prize
It is a new day, the battle has been won
Hallelujah, Hallelujah to the Son!

When I could not see, You instructed
me to walk by your word,
And not be moved by what I see
When everything in this world opposed me like a flood,
You told me to stand my ground in you,
and know that you will fight for me

In the midst of trials and tribulations I stood alone
But you assured me you were with me
and would not forsake me
When I thought I could never make it
You hid me under the shadow of your
wings until it was safe to release me.

For in the day of trouble he will keep me safe in his dwelling;
he will hide me in the shelter of his tabernacle and set me
high upon a rock." Psalm 27:5

POEM REFLECTION
Torrents Of A Soaring River

How did this poem and scripture speak to me?

PRAYER: Holy Spirit, make me aware of the changes needed in my life, then give me the mind and strength to follow through. Thank you, Holy Spirit, for your footprints.

LIST CHANGES TO BE MADE
**Revealed areas of my life by the
Holy Spirit to make changes**

Emancipation

The innermost parts of my soul praise you,
O God, my Lord, and my Savior
My spirit leaps to heights unimaginable
To the naked eye I appear, out of my mind
O my God, to say You are Worthy to be Praised -
is still to act in ignorance of our human capacity
But with all that I am, there are no words to
truly describe the reality of who you are
Oh my God, I bow down in spirit,
soul and body to Your Majesty
My God, My Lord and My Savior

Thank you could never suffice for all you have done for me
Let me scream it from the mountain top
and the depths of the deepest sea
In the configurations of the heavens and all the earth
You are God, and beside you there is none other
Let the heavens and the earth proclaim Your Glory
In Majesty that is due only to Your Name
Thank you God for making me whole!

"Let everything that has breath, praise the Lord. Praise the
Lord" Psalm 150:6

POEM REFLECTION
Emancipation

How did this poem and scripture speak to me?

PRAYER: Holy Spirit, make me aware of the changes needed in my life, then give me the mind and strength to follow through. Thank you, Holy Spirit, for your footprints.

LIST CHANGES TO BE MADE
**Revealed areas of my life by the
Holy Spirit to make changes**

Transformational Grace

Although we agree to submit our will,
We haven't the faintest clue of what He will do
Over a period of time, with fear and
anxiety, we finally make the leap
Holding on for dear life because we've
never walked this way before
Each step is an adventure
An adventure that leads us into more
and more unfamiliar ground
Sometimes the struggle to continue
seems more than we can bear
Yet, there is a place within the unfamiliarity when
enough strength and courage is given to continue

I have come to realize, it is a place of resolve,
though I cannot adequately explain
Something happens from within -
continuously revealing growth
A growth that until now could not even be fathomed
How awesome to see the changes occur
Even though at times, the struggles are severe
I've learnt through the process to rest in Him
He is taking me from grace to grace as He transforms me
How can I witness to a love so real, except to
say, it is Your Transformational Grace!

I stand in awe of His mighty presence
A presence which dictates, I am not in control
While my flesh and my spirit war one against the other

His presence brings assurance – He is in control
Though the battle rages deep within my soul,
there is a presence that fights to be released
Like a roaring Lion it paces and roars to be free
Overcoming the fear of bondage and the bars of my cage
I strained to occupy the territory of
promise for which is mine
Bursting from my prison, Alas! I felt at home
My perception had become clear, my joy without limits
Alas, my soul had become free
Transformational Grace has overtaken me!

"Trust in the Lord with all your heart and lean not on your own understanding; in all your ways acknowledge him, and he will make your paths straight." Proverbs 3:5-6

POEM REFLECTION
Transformational Grace

How did this poem and scripture speak to me?

PRAYER: Holy Spirit, make me aware of the changes needed in my life, then give me the mind and strength to follow through. Thank you, Holy Spirit, for your footprints.

LIST CHANGES TO BE MADE
Revealed areas of my life by the
Holy Spirit to make changes

Born To Be Free But Lived In A Cage

Born to be free but lived in a cage
Trapped by an unregenerate mind and spirit
being sorely ruled by the flesh and others
How dangerous and explosive a situation
When all the capacity to 'Be' is present
But without a knowledge of truth
We exist being less than we aught

We struggle through life as if pacing in a cage
While the intent is to be free and explore all there is to be -
We are bound and limited
By instinct we know there has to be more
But the mind and spirit are trapped and
needs enlightening to be free

Who will the trainers be – where are they we ask?
Where do we receive the kind of nourishment
that prepares us to be free?
We wrestle with discontentment inside
Tired of being in a cage – not knowing how to get out
Are we enslaved by circumstances,
conditions, people or even ourselves?
Whatever the case we must be free
Alas! Out of sheer torment and frustration,
the mind is made up - to be free
Not knowing how or what to do, a resolve is made

Out of nowhere came help when the resolution was made
This began the journey of freedom to
live the life that is meant to be
With a mighty thug, the bars of the
cage came crashing down
It was as though life had come for the first time
The awakening that thoughts are powerful in any situation
Brings with it an understanding of a
choice to be forever bound or free
Oh the smell of all the new possibilities yet to be explored
Run, yes run in this freedom, Dance, fly - And
Be all you are meant to be!

"Do not conform any longer to the pattern of this world, but be transformed by the renewing of your mind. Then you will be able to test and approve what God's will is – his good, pleasing and perfect will." Romans 12:2

POEM REFLECTION
Born To Be Free But Lived In A Cage

How did this poem and scripture speak to me?

PRAYER: Holy Spirit, make me aware of the changes needed in my life, then give me the mind and strength to follow through. Thank you, Holy Spirit, for your footprints.

LIST CHANGES TO BE MADE
**Revealed areas of my life by the
Holy Spirit to make changes**

Dare To Believe

The entire journey is one of faith - motivated by love
Faith to believe what you cannot see but
in your spirit you know to be truth
Faith to act on that belief even when it
contradicts what is logic to everyone else
And even your own common sense and feelings
Faith to surrender yourself, circumstances,
conditions and those whom you love -
To the One who knows all
And Faith to hold on when your back is up against
the wall and you cannot see your way through

You suddenly realize, you are not utterly in
charge, no matter how hard you try
Some things are beyond your control

Coming to this realization, be willing to
accept the help you cannot give yourself
Oh, what do you have to lose? Nothing, only to gain
I dare you, try the One who knitted you together,
gave you life and a purpose for a specific plan
A plan to prosper you and give you eternal life
Put your trust in Him and you shall see
A life beyond comparison of what
you ever thought it could be
DARE TO BELIEVE!

"For you created my innermost being; you knit me together
in my mother's womb. Your eyes saw my unformed body. All
the days ordained for me were written in your book before
one of them came to be." Psalm 139:13,16

POEM REFLECTION
Dare To Believe

How did this poem and scripture speak to me?

PRAYER: Holy Spirit, make me aware of the changes needed in my life, then give me the mind and strength to follow through. Thank you, Holy Spirit, for your footprints.

LIST CHANGES TO BE MADE
**Revealed areas of my life by the
Holy Spirit to make changes**

Sacrifice Is Eminent To Reaping The Harvest

In our, want-it-now systems of the natural world
It's a given for many to want to glean the
harvest without investing in the soil
Dirtying the hands is not in the plan and
cultivating the soil is not an option
Left without a watchman, thieves come
in to kill, steal and destroy
But - the natural instinct is to glean without sacrifice
How absurd, harvest comes only after
the sacrifice of planting!

Receiving the harvest calls for an all-out
strategy of discipline, determination,
and keeping our eyes on the prize
To lose sight of the prize weakens the
overall position of success
A determination must be there to really want it, have
to have it or, plain and simple, can't live without it
Taking inventory of our strengths and weaknesses,
we ready ourselves to execute a plan -
of action highlighting, 'Sacrifice'

With help from the Master, hindering
agents to the harvest are eliminated
In our own strength, we are limited - but
Realizing the task at hand is subject
to the Lord of the harvest
At the appointed time, reaping is eminent, if we do not faint
If we faint not, we will reap the harvest

SACRIFICE IS EMINENT TO
REAPING THE HARVEST!

"Let us not become weary in doing good, for at the proper
time we will reap a harvest if we do not give up." Galatians 6:9

POEM REFLECTION
Sacrifice Is Eminent To Reaping The Harvest

How did this poem and scripture speak to me?

PRAYER: Holy Spirit, make me aware of the changes needed in my life, then give me the mind and strength to follow through. Thank you, Holy Spirit, for your footprints.

LIST CHANGES TO BE MADE
**Revealed areas of my life by the
Holy Spirit to make changes**

Poured Out Like A Cup Overflowing

Poured out like a cup overflowing is to live a sacrificial life
A life where -
Moving beyond our soulish nature, we allow
the Spirit of God to take control
A choice is made to be co-laborers
with Christ- fit for His service
Not that we have arrived but that we
yield to the Master's will
His grace and mercy is sufficient to
make us pliable for service

With hearts and hands ready to serve, we
are subject to the Master's bidding
Ours is to be open to our Loving Father who will
instruct us to pour out into the lives of others
What a privilege to be used by the Master!
It's nothing we could have worked
for, earned or is entitled to
But because of His love, grace and mercy, He
has seen fit to make all who would –
Joint heirs and co-laborers with Jesus Christ

How exhilarating - in a selfish world, to be poured
out like a cup overflowing, being the hands, and
feet of Jesus, opting to reach the holistic person
To generate hope with the intent of making it come
alive within the hearts and minds of the despondent

To encourage and support by prodding those who
cannot find the strength on their own to rise to action
To generate contagious enthusiasm inciting the
downtrodden and despondent to vision, will and action
And yes, to carry the message of the Good News
of Jesus Christ that none need be lost!

Poured out like a cup overflowing is to live life in its fullest
There is no greater joy than to offer the
gift of Christ that keeps on giving
TO BE POURED OUT LIKE A CUP OVERFLOWING!

"For we are God's workmanship, created in Christ Jesus to do
good works, which God prepared in advance for us to do."
Ephesians 2:10

POEM REFLECTION
Poured Out Like A Cup Overflowing

How did this poem and scripture speak to me?

PRAYER: Holy Spirit, make me aware of the changes needed in my life, then give me the mind and strength to follow through. Thank you, Holy Spirit, for your footprints.

LIST CHANGES TO BE MADE
**Revealed areas of my life by the
Holy Spirit to make changes**

Prayer

Wars, rumors of wars within or without
– Prayer is our weapon to fight
A weapon of defense so mighty indeed - God
comes to our rescue and meets our need
We need not be afraid, with Him by our side
He's never lost a battle and is our guide
Engaged in our fight - demons flee
God will surely bring us - victory

Strategically placed, we receive His grace
To fight every battle and run every race
Through prayer we survive in His loving embrace
And see our enemies removed without a trace
Though the enemy be revealed as a stallion so strong
Our God will diminish him like a pawn
Prayer likened to a lasso decisively released
Apprehends the neck of the thundering
beast - bringing defeat
Be not afraid of his statue and pace
We have the Living Word and stand in God's Grace

"For though we live in the world, we do not wage war as the
world does. The weapons we fight with are not the weapons
of the world. On the contrary, they have divine power to
demolish strongholds." 2 Corinthians 10:3-4

POEM REFLECTION
Prayer

How did this poem and scripture speak to me?

PRAYER: Holy Spirit, make me aware of the changes needed in my life, then give me the mind and strength to follow through. Thank you, Holy Spirit, for your footprints.

LIST CHANGES TO BE MADE
Revealed areas of my life by the
Holy Spirit to make changes

90

Summary Of Findings

Use the chart below to document the "changes to be made" as revealed to you by the Holy Spirit during your Poem Reflections. Begin with your first response and continue to record subsequent responses for each poem reflection. Pay close attention to the Footprints of the Holy Spirit and be intentional to His guidance in your life. Upon concluding your "Summary of Findings" be sure to share your testimony.

FOOTPRINTS OF THE HOLY SPIRIT
LOOK TO THE SOURCE:
A LETTER TO GOD:
A CRY FOR HELP:

THE BEAUTY OF A ROSE:

LIFE IS A JOURNEY:

THE NAKED TRUTH:

THE JOURNEY:

HOPE:

MY GUIDE:

A VALLEY OF INDECISION:

MIRACLE OF THE DOCK:

REALIZATION:

WHO AM I?:

A BLESSED PROMISE:

THE MIRACLE OF A SEED:

COME INTO THE DEEP:

STAND FIRM IN THE STORM:

MAKE A CHOICE:

DESTINED TO SOAR AS AN EAGLE:

PERCEPTION OF THE BITTER PILL:

GRATEFUL:

FAVOR OF THE DIVINE:

TORRENTS OF A SOARING RIVER:

EMANCIPATION:

TRANSFORMATIONAL GRACE:

BORN TO BE FREE BUT LIVE IN A CAGE:

DARE TO BELIEVE:

SACRIFICE IS EMINENT TO REAPING THE HARVEST:

POURED OUT LIKE A CUP OVERFLOWING:
PRAYER:

Jesus said "But I, when I am lifted up from the earth, [I] will draw all [people] to myself." John 12:32

Prayer Of Gratitude

Gracious and loving Father,
You and you alone deserve all the praise,
all the glory and all the honor
O how you love your children
Your loving kindness, grace and mercy all wrapped in love
Seeks, draws, cleanse, prepares, and
lavishes us with your amazing favor
Blessed be your name forever and ever!

Who is like unto you O Lord?
You've given your word to hide in the depths of our souls
Your many promises sustain while
you're making us like pure gold
You lead, guide and correct
And when the season is right - you lift and promote

Who can open a door when you shut it - Or
Who can shut a door when you open it?
You shut the doors to preserve us from our enemy
You open the door when the enemy tries to subdue us
And you set us free
Oh how glorious it is to finally see
Your tapestry in full harmony!

Prayer For Salvation

(9) "…If you confess with your mouth, 'Jesus is Lord,' and believe in your heart that God raised him from the dead, you will be saved." (10) "For it is with your heart that you believe and are justified, and it is with your mouth that you confess and are saved" (Romans 10:9-10).

> Lord Jesus, open my eyes to see you
> My mouth to confess you
> And
> My heart to receive and experience you
> Forgive me for my sins
> Now, I accept Jesus as my personal
> Savior, and my personal Lord
> Receive my life to give you praise, glory, and honor
> In Jesus name
> Amen!

Name _____

Date _____

If you prayed this prayer and meant it in your heart, you are now a born again child of God. Welcome to the family of believers worldwide!

About the Author

Sandra Hadland has been engaged in ministry for over twenty years and is the special assistant to the pastor of the First Baptist Church of Stratford, Stratford, Connecticut. In this role, she seeks to provide pastoral care to those entrusted to her. Over the years, she has been actively engaged in various aspects of ministry within the Baptist denomination, to include President of the American Baptist Churches of Connecticut (ABCCONN). Her passion though is not constrained to denomination but building the kingdom of God.

Sandra is actively involved in preaching, teaching, facilitating workshops, and public speaking, mentoring the young and old alike. Over the years, her Christ-centered passion has been intentionally committed to evoking an insatiable hunger and thirst for Christ by generating enthusiasm that will become contagious to incite the downtrodden and despondent to vision, will and action. It is out of the experiences of ministry and life's daily encounters, coupled with a dynamic radical passion to help others, that Sandra intentionally chose to take her ministry beyond the four walls of the church building to wherever the Holy Spirit would lead. She is receptive and committed to building one life at a time, as is witnessed by her book of poems *Transformational Grace, a language of the transforming power of God's grace through poetry*.

Sandra is a native of Nassau, Bahamas and the mother of three sons, Sidney, Julian and Robert, and has nine grandchildren and three great grand children. For more information, please visit her website at www.SandraHadland.com.

CPSIA information can be obtained
at www.ICGtesting.com
Printed in the USA
LVHW050421180122
708477LV00020B/894

9 781640 880894